HIS HOUR

THE SACRED HEART OF JESUS . . . began this devotion of the Holy Hour of Reparation, when He entered the Garden of Gethsemani on Mount Olivet. He said to His Apostles: "My soul is sorrowful even unto death. Stay you here and watch with Me." Later He said to them: "Could you not watch one hour with Me? Watch and pray, that you enter not into temptation." (Matt. XXVI. 38, 40, 41.)

As Jesus spoke to His Apostles, so He pleads with us to stay and watch and pray with Him. His Sacred Heart is filled with sadness, because so many doubt Him, despise Him, insult Him, ridicule Him, spit upon Him, slap Him, accuse Him, condemn Him. In the Sacrament of His Love, so many forget Him. Every mortal sin brings down the terrible scourges on His Sacred Body, presses the sharp thorns into His Sacred Head, and hammers the cruel nails into His Sacred Hands and Feet. The ingratitude of mankind continually pierces His Sacred Heart.

When Jesus saw the sins of the world and the reparation that must be made to His Heavenly Father, He began to fear and to be sad and sorrowful. "Kneeling down, He prayed: 'Father, if Thou will, remove this chalice from Me; But not My Will, Thine be done.' There appeared an angel from heaven to strengthen Him; and being in agony, He prayed the longer, and His sweat became as drops of blood trickling to the ground." (Luke. XXII. 41, 44.)

The Sacred Heart of Jesus said to St. Margaret Mary: "Make reparation for the ingratitude of men. Spend an hour in prayer to appease divine justice, to implore mercy for sinners, to honor Me, to console Me for My bitter suffering when abandoned by My Apostles, when they did not WATCH ONE HOUR WITH ME."

In the Name of the Father,✛ and of the Son, and of the Holy Spirit. Amen.

(Here make the Intention for the Holy Hour)

All:—

O Sacrament most holy, * O Sacrament divine!
   * All praise and all thanksgiving * be every moment Thine!

Leader:—
PRAYER TO THE HOLY SPIRIT
All:—

Come, O Holy Spirit, * fill the hearts of Thy faithful * and enkindle in them the fire of Thy love. * Send forth Thy Spirit, * and they shall be created, * and Thou shalt renew the face of the earth. *

O God, * Who by the light of the Holy Spirit, * didst instruct the hearts of the faithful, * grant that in the same Holy Spirit * we may be truly wise, * and ever rejoice in His consolation. * Through Christ our Lord. * Amen. *

Heart of Jesus, * I put my trust in Thee!

Leader:—
ACT OF CONTRITION
All:—

O my God! * I am heartily sorry for having offended Thee, * and I detest all my sins, * because I dread the loss of heaven and the pains of hell, * but most of all because they offend Thee, * my God, * Who art all-good * and deserving of all my love.

* I firmly resolve, * with the help of Thy grace, * to confess my sins, * to do penance, * and to amend my life. * Amen. *

> O *Jesus in the Blessed Sacrament,**
> *have mercy on us!*

Leader:—
ACT OF SPIRITUAL COMMUNION
All:—

m y Jesus, * I believe that Thou art really present * in the most Blessed Sacrament of the Altar. * I love Thee above everything else, * and I long to receive Thee into my soul. * I cannot now receive Thee in Holy Communion, * but I beg Thee * to come to me at least spiritually. * I embrace Thee as already there, * and unite myself entirely to Thee. * Grant that I may never be separated from Thee! *

> I *adore Thee every moment,* *
> *O Living Bread from heaven,* *
> *Great Sacrament!*

OFFERING OF THE HOLY HOUR
All:—

m y Sweet Jesus, * I desire to spend this Hour with Thee, * to console Thee, * and to make some reparation by the love of my poor heart * for the agony Thou didst suffer in Gethsemani. * In that lone hour Thou wast forsaken, * and the creatures, whom Thou didst create to love Thee, * loved Thee not. * The weight of all our sins pressed on Thee, * and mine as well; * and for the sorrow * which I caused Thee then by my sins, * I will endeavor

* to repay Thee now by my love. * Strengthen it,
* my Jesus, * that it may in some small measure
* give Thee consolation. *

——— ✠ ———

S *acred Heart of Jesus,* * *strengthened in Thine
agony by an Angel,* * *comfort us in our agony.*

Leader:—
        OPENING PRAYER TO THE BLESSED
All:—   SACRAMENT

m y Lord Jesus Christ, * it is Thy great love for
      men * that keeps Thee day and night in this
Sacrament, * full of pity and love, * expecting, *
inviting, * and welcoming all who visit Thee. * I
believe that Thou art * really present * in the
Sacrament of the Altar. * From the depth of my noth-
ingness, * I adore Thee; * and I thank Thee *
for the many graces Thou hast given me, * especially * for the gift of Thyself in this Sacrament, *
for the gift of Thy most holy Mother * as my in-
tercessor, * and for the privilege * of visiting
Thee in this Church. *

I now speak to Thy most loving Heart * with a
three-fold intention: * to thank Thee for the great
gift of Thyself; * to atone for all the insults *
which Thy enemies heap upon Thee in this Sacrament; * and to adore Thee * wherever Thy Eucharistic Presence * is dishonored or forgotten. *

My Jesus, * I love Thee with my whole heart. *
I am very sorry for my ingratitude * to Thy infinite
goodness. * I now resolve, * with the help of Thy
grace, * never to offend Thee again. * And, sin-

ful as I am, * I consecrate to Thee * my entire self, * my whole will, * my affections, * my desires, * and all that I have. * From now on, * do with me and mine * as Thou pleasest. * I ask for and desire only Thy love, * final perseverance, * and the grace always to do Thy holy will. *

I intercede with Thee for the souls in purgatory, * especially for those * who were most devoted to the Blessed Sacrament, * and to Thy most holy Mother. * I recommend to Thee also, * all poor sinners. * And lastly, * my dear Savior, * I unite all my desires * with the desires of Thy most loving Heart. * Thus united, * I present them to Thy Eternal Father, * and beg Him in Thy Name * and for love of Thee, * to hear and answer them. *

St. Alphonsus M. de'Liguori

*Jesus, meek and humble of heart, * make our hearts like unto Thine.*

Leader:—   ACT OF FAITH
All:—

O my God! * I firmly believe all the sacred truths * which Thy holy Catholic Church * believes and teaches, * because Thou hast revealed them, * Who canst neither deceive * nor be deceived.

Leader:—   ACT OF HOPE
All:—

O my God! * Relying on Thy infinite goodness and promises, * I hope to obtain the pardon of my sins, * the assistance of Thy grace, * and life ever-lasting, * through the merits of Jesus Christ, * our Lord and Savior.

Leader:—

ACT OF LOVE

All:—

O my God! * I love Thee above all things * with my whole heart and soul, * because Thou art all-good, * and worthy of all love. * I love my neighbor as myself * for the love of Thee. * I forgive all who have injured me, * and ask pardon of all whom I have injured. *

> *Jesus, I live for Thee, * Jesus, I die for Thee; * Jesus, I am thine in life and in death. Amen.*

Leader:—

ACT OF CHARITY

All:—

O good and merciful Savior, * it is the desire of my heart * to return Thee love for love. * My greatest sorrow is * that Thou art not loved by all men, * and, in particular, * that my heart is so cold, * so selfish, * so ungrateful. * Deeply sensible of my own weakness and poverty, * I trust that Thy own grace * will enable me to offer Thee * an act of pure love. * And I wish to offer Thee * this act of love * in reparation for the coldness and neglect * that are shown to Thee * in the Sacrament of Thy love * by Thy creatures. * O Jesus, my sovereign good, * I love Thee, * not for the sake of the reward which Thou hast promised * to those who love Thee, * but purely for Thyself. * I love Thee * above all things that can be loved, * above all pleasures, * and in fine * above myself and all that is not Thee, * protesting in the presence of heaven and earth * that I will live and die * purely and simply in Thy holy love, * and that if to love Thee thus * I must endure persecution and suffering, * I am perfectly satisfied, * and I will ever say with St. Paul: * "Nothing shall separate me * from the love of Christ." *

O Jesus, * Supreme Master of all hearts, * I love Thee, * I adore Thee, * I praise Thee, * I thank Thee, * because I am now all Thine own. * Rule over me, * and transform my soul * into the likeness of Thyself, * so that it may bless and glorify Thee * forever in the abode of the Saints. * Amen. * ——— * ———

S weet heart of Jesus, * have mercy on us and on our erring brethren.

Leader:—
PRAYER TO CHRIST THE KING

All:—
O Christ Jesus, * I acknowledge Thee King of the Universe. * All that has been made * has been created for Thee. * Make full use of Thy rights over me. * I renew the promises I made in Baptism, * when I renounced Satan * and all his pomps and works, * and I promise to live a good Christian life;

* and especially I undertake to help, * to the extent of my means, * to secure the triumph of the rights of God * and of Thy Church. * Divine Heart of Jesus, * I offer Thee my efforts to obtain that all hearts * may acknowledge Thy Sacred Royalty, * and that so the Kingdom of Thy peace * may be established * throughout the entire universe. * Amen. *

Jesus, * King and Center of all hearts, * through the advent of Thy Kingdom, * grant us peace.

Leader:—

LITANY OF THE SACRED HEART OF JESUS

Leader:— Lord, have mercy on us.
All:— Christ, have mercy on us.
Leader:— Lord, have mercy on us. Christ, hear us.
All:— Christ, graciously hear us.
Leader:— God, the Father of Heaven,
All:— Have mercy on us.

God, the Son, Redeemer of the world,
God, the Holy Spirit,
Holy Trinity, one God,
Heart of Jesus, Son of the Eternal Father,
Heart of Jesus, formed by the Holy Spirit in the Womb of the Virgin Mother,
Heart of Jesus, substantially united to the Word of God,
Heart of Jesus, of Infinite Majesty,
Heart of Jesus, Holy Temple of God,

— Have mercy on us —

Heart of Jesus, Tabernacle of the Most High,
Heart of Jesus, House of God and Gate of Heaven,
Heart of Jesus, burning furnace of Charity,
Heart of Jesus, abode of Justice and Love,
Heart of Jesus, full of Goodness and Love,
Heart of Jesus, abyss of all virtues,
Heart of Jesus, most worthy of all praise,
Heart of Jesus, King and Center of all hearts,
Heart of Jesus, in Whom are all the treasures
    of wisdom and knowledge,
Heart of Jesus, in Whom dwells the fullness
    of Divinity,
Heart of Jesus, in Whom the Father was well
    pleased,
Heart of Jesus, of Whose fullness we have
    all received,
Heart of Jesus, desire of the everlasting hills,
Heart of Jesus, patient and most merciful,
Heart of Jesus, enriching all who invoke Thee,
Heart of Jesus, fountain of life and holiness,
Heart of Jesus, propitiation for our sins,
Heart of Jesus, loaded down with reproaches,
Heart of Jesus, bruised for our offences,
Heart of Jesus, obedient unto death,
Heart of Jesus, pierced with a lance,
Heart of Jesus, source of all consolation,
Heart of Jesus, our life and resurrection,
Heart of Jesus, our peace and reconciliation,
Heart of Jesus, Victim for sin,

Have mercy on us

Have mercy on us

Heart of Jesus, salvation of those who trust in Thee,

Heart of Jesus, hope of those who die in Thee,

Heart of Jesus, delight of all the Saints,

Leader:— Lamb of God, Who takest away the sins of the world,

All:— Spare us, O Lord.

Leader:— Lamb of God, Who takest away the sins of the world,

All:— Graciously hear us, O Lord.

Leader:— Lamb of God, Who takest away the sins of the world,

All:— Have mercy on us.

Leader:— Jesus meek and humble of Heart,

All:— Make our hearts like unto Thine.

Leader:— LET US PRAY:—O Almighty and Eternal God, look upon the Heart of Thy dearly beloved Son, and upon the praise and satisfaction He offers Thee in the name of sinners and for those who seek Thy mercy; be Thou appeased, and grant us pardon in the name of the same Jesus Christ, Thy Son, Who liveth and reigneth with Thee, in the unity of the Holy Spirit, world without end.

All:— Amen. *

S acred Heart of Jesus, * I believe in Thy love for me.

Leader:—

CONSECRATION OF THE HUMAN RACE
TO THE SACRED HEART OF JESUS

Ordered by His Holiness, Pope Pius XI, Dec. 11, 1925. For One Fold and One Shepherd.

All:—

most Sweet Jesus, * Redeemer of the human race, * look down upon us humbly prostrate before Thee. * We are Thine and Thine we wish to be; * but to be more surely united with Thee, * behold each one of us freely consecrates himself to-day * to Thy Most Sacred Heart. *

Many indeed have never known Thee; * many, too, despising Thy precepts, * have rejected Thee. * Have mercy on them all, most merciful Jesus, * and draw them to Thy Sacred Heart. * Be Thou King, O Lord, * not only of the faithful who have never forsaken Thee, * but also of the prodigal children who have abandoned Thee. * Grant that they may quickly return to their Father's house * lest they die of wretchedness and hunger. *

Be Thou King of those who are deceived by erroneous opinions, * or whom discord keeps aloof, * and call them back to the harbor of truth and unity of faith, * so that soon there may be * but one flock and one Shepherd. *

Grant, O Lord, to Thy Church, * assurance of freedom and immunity from harm; * give peace and order to all nations, * and make the earth resound, * from pole to pole with one cry: * Praise to the Divine Heart * that wrought our salvation; * to It be glory and honor forever. * Amen. *

S acred Heart of Jesus, * Thy Kingdom come!

Leader:— ACT OF REPARATION

All:—

O Sacred Heart of Jesus, * animated with a desire * to repair the outrages unceasingly offered to Thee, * we prostrate before Thy throne of mercy, * and in the name of all mankind, * pledge our love and fidelity to Thee! *

The more Thy mysteries are blasphemed, * the more firmly we shall believe them, * O Sacred Heart of Jesus! *

The more impiety endeavors to extinguish our hopes of immortality, * the more we shall trust in Thy Heart, * sole hope of mankind! *

The more hearts resist Thy Divine attractions, * the more we shall love Thee, * O infinitely amiable Heart of Jesus! *

The more unbelief attacks Thy Divinity, * the

more humbly and profoundly we shall adore It, * O Divine Heart of Jesus! *

The more Thy holy laws are transgressed and ignored, * the more we shall delight to observe them, * O most holy Heart of Jesus! *

The more Thy Sacraments are despised and abandoned, * the more frequently we shall receive them with love and reverence, * O most liberal Heart of Jesus! *

The more the imitation of Thy virtues is neglected and forgotten, * the more we shall endeavor to practice them, * O Heart, model of every virtue! *

The more the devil labors to destroy souls, * the more we shall be inflamed with desire to save them, * O Heart of Jesus, zealous Lover of souls! *

The more sin and impurity destroy the image of God in man, * the more we shall try by purity of life * to be a living temple of the Holy Spirit, * O Heart of Jesus! *

The more Thy Holy Church is despised, * the more we shall endeavor * to be her faithful children, * O Sweet Heart of Jesus! *

The more Thy Vicar on earth is persecuted, * the more will we honor him * as the infallible head of Thy Holy Church, * show our fidelity and pray for him, * O kingly Heart of Jesus! *

O Sacred Heart, * through Thy powerful grace, may we become Thy apostles * in the midst of a corrupted world, * and be Thy crown in the kingdom of heaven. * Amen. *

——— ✠ ———

P raise and adoration ever more be given *
to the most holy Sacrament!

—— * ——

THE HOLY ROSARY

Leader:—

THE APOSTLES' CREED

I believe in God, * the Father Almighty, * Creator
of heaven and earth; * and in Jesus Christ, * His
only Son, * our Lord; * Who was conceived by the
Holy Spirit, * born of the Virgin Mary, * suffered
under Pontius Pilate, * was crucified; * died, and
was buried. * He descended into hell; * the third
day He arose again from the dead; * He ascended into heaven, * sitteth at the right hand of God, the
Father Almighty; * from thence He shall come * to
judge the living and the dead. *

All:—

I believe in the Holy Spirit, * the holy Catholic
Church, * the communion of Saints, * the for-
giveness of sins, * the resurrection of the body, *
and life everlasting. * Amen.

1 Our Father — 3 Hail Marys — 1 Glory be to the Father, etc.

Leader:—

THE SORROWFUL MYSTERIES

The First Sorrowful Mystery—
The Agony of Jesus in the Garden.

" **m** y soul is sorrowful unto death!" O divine sadness of Jesus, Who savest the world and preparest for us the joys of Paradise, heal all our sorrows, accept our sorrow for having so greatly offended the Lord our God!

1 Our Father — 10 Hail Marys — 1 Glory be to the Father, etc.

Leader:— ALL STAND.

The Second Sorrowful Mystery— Jesus is Scourged at the Pillar.

" **m** y people, what have I done to you? Wherein have I offended you? Laden with My gifts you scourge Me like the least of slaves!" O Jesus, forgive the excesses of impiety against the Church, Thy mystic body!

1 Our Father — 10 Hail Marys — 1 Glory be to the Father, etc.

Leader:—

The Third Sorrowful Mystery— Jesus is Crowned with Thorns.

" **I** am a worm and no man!" O Jesus, sated with outrages in this Mystery, with what eloquence dost Thou not show us that, lifted up from earth, we ever return to it again! May this divine lesson subdue our pride!

1 Our Father – 10 Hail Marys – 1 Glory be to the Father, etc.

Leader:—

The Fourth Sorrowful Mystery—
Jesus Carries His Cross.

"They forced the Cyrenean to take up His Cross."
Each day we also receive our crosses from Thy hand. O Jesus, grant that we may carry them, not by force, but for love.

1 Our Father — 10 Hail Marys — 1 Glory be to the Father, etc

Leader:— ALL KNEEL.

The Fifth Sorrowful Mystery—
Jesus Dies on the Cross.

"Behold thy Mother!" I thank Thee, O my Savior, for this admirable gift, this last will of Thy love. Grant that I may respond to it by a generous love toward Thy afflicted Mother.

1 Our Father — 10 Hail Marys — 1 Glory be to the Father, etc.

Leader:—
HAIL, HOLY QUEEN
All:—

Hail, Holy Queen, * Mother of mercy, * our life, * our sweetness, * and our hope! * To thee do we cry, * poor banished children of Eve; * to thee do we send up our sighs, * mourning and weeping in this valley of tears. * Turn then, * most gracious advocate, * thine eyes of mercy toward us, * and after this our exile, * show unto us the blessed fruit of thy womb, Jesus. * O clement, * O loving, * O sweet Virgin Mary.

Leader:— Pray for us, O Queen of the most holy Rosary.

All:— That we may be made worthy * of the promises of Christ.

Leader:— LET US PRAY:—O God, * Whose only-begotten Son, * by His life, death, and resurrection, * has purchased for us * the rewards of eternal salvation; * grant, we beseech Thee, * that meditating upon these mysteries * in the most holy Rosary of the Blessed Virgin Mary, * we may imitate what they contain, * and obtain what they promise. * Through the same Christ our Lord.

All:— Amen. *

L ord, I thank Thee, * that Thou didst die on the Cross * for my sins.

Leader:—

TO THE QUEEN OF THE HOLY ROSARY
All:—

O Queen of the most holy Rosary, * in these times of brazen impiety, * show again thy power, * with the signs which accompanied thy victories of old, * and from the throne where thou art seated, * dispensing pardon and grace, * in pity watch over the Church of thy Son, * His Vicar, * and every order of the clergy and laity, * suffering in grievous warfare. * Hasten, * O most powerful destroyer of heresy, * hasten the hour of mercy, * seeing that the hour of judgment * is daily challenged by innumerable offences. * Obtain for me, * the lowest of men, * kneeling suppliant in thy presence, * the grace which may enable me to live * a just life on earth, * and reign with the just in heaven, * whilst with the faithful throughout the world, * O Queen of the most holy Rosary, * I salute thee and cry out: * Queen of the most holy Rosary, * pray for us! *

*Sacred Heart of Jesus, * I give myself to Thee * through Mary.*

Leader:—

TO JESUS ABANDONED

All:—

With Mary Immaculate, * let us adore, thank, implore and console, * the Most Beloved and Sacred Heart of Jesus * in the Blessed Sacrament. *

O Divine Jesus, * lonely tonight in so many Tabernacles, * without visitor or worshipper * I offer Thee my poor heart. * May its every throb be an act of love for Thee. * Thou art always watching beneath the Sacramental Veils; * in Thy Love Thou dost never sleep * and Thou art never weary * of Thy vigil for sinners. * O lonely Jesus, * may the flame of my heart * burn and beam always in company with Thee. *

*O Sacrament most holy, * O Sacrament divine! * All praise and all thanksgiving * be every moment Thine!*

Leader:—

VENERATION OF THE THORN-CROWNED HEAD OF THE SAVIOR

All:—

And platting a crown of thorns, * they put it up-on His head. * They began to spit upon Him, * and they gave Him blows. * Others smote His face and said:* "Prophesy, * who is it that struck Thee? "

O holy Redeemer! * Thou art clothed with a scarlet cloak, * a reed is placed in Thy hands for a sceptre, * and the sharp points of a thorny crown * are pressed into Thy adorable head. *

My soul, * thou canst never conceive the suffer-ings, * the insults and indignities offered to our Blessed Lord * during this scene of pain and mockery. *

I therefore salute Thee and offer Thee supreme homage * as King of heaven and earth, * the Redeemer of the world, * the Eternal Son of the living God. *

O my afflicted Savior! * O King of the world,* Thou art ridiculed as a mock king. * I believe in Thee and adore Thee * as the King of kings and Lord of lords, * as the supreme Ruler of heaven and earth. *

O Jesus! * I devoutly venerate Thy sacred head pierced with thorns, * struck with a reed, * over-whelmed with pain and derision. *

I adore the Precious Blood * flowing from Thy bleeding wounds. * To Thee be all praise, * all thanksgiving * and all love for evermore. *

O meek Lamb, * Victim for sin! * May Thy thorns * penetrate my heart with fervent love, * that I may never cease to adore Thee as my God, * my King and my Savior.

Leader:— Behold, O God, our Protector,

All:— And look upon the face of Thy Christ.

Leader:— LET US PRAY:—O my beloved Savior, at sight of Thy most holy face disfigured by suffering, at sight of Thy Sacred Heart so full of love, I cry out with St. Augustine: "Lord Jesus, imprint on my heart Thy sacred wounds, so that I may read therein sorrow and love: sorrow, to endure every sorrow for Thee; love, to despise every love for Thee."

All:— Amen. *

———— * ————

W *e adore Thee, * O Christ, * and we bless Thee, * because by Thy holy Cross * Thou hast redeemed the world.*

Leader:—

TO OUR LORD ON THE CROSS

All:—

M y Crucified Jesus, * mercifully accept the prayer * which I now make to Thee * for help in the moment of my death, * when at its approach * all my senses shall fail me. *

When, therefore, O sweetest Jesus, * my weary and downcast eyes * can no longer look up to Thee, * be mindful of the loving gaze * which I now turn on Thee, * and have mercy on me. *

When my parched lips * can no longer kiss Thy most sacred wounds, * remember then those kisses * which now I imprint on Thee, * and have mercy on me. *

When my cold hands * can no longer embrace Thy Cross, * forget not the affection * with which I embrace it now, * and have mercy on me. *

And when, at length, * my swollen and lifeless tongue * can no longer speak, * remember that I called upon Thee now. *

Jesus, Mary, Joseph, * to you I commend my soul. * Amen. *

E ternal Father, * I offer Thee the Wounds * of our Lord Jesus Christ * to heal the wounds of our souls.

Leader:—
DEVOTION IN HONOR OF THE FIVE
HOLY WOUNDS
All:—

A s I kneel before Thee on the Cross, * most loving Savior of my soul, * my conscience tells me it is I * who have nailed Thee to that Cross * with these hands of mine, * as often as I have fallen into mortal sin, * wearying Thee with my monstrous ingratitude. *

My God, * my chief and most perfect Good, * worthy of all my love, * seeing Thou hast ever loaded me with blessings, * I cannot now undo my misdeeds, * as I would most willingly, * but I can

and will loathe them, * grieving greatly for having
offended Thee * Who art infinite Goodness. * And
now, * kneeling at Thy feet, * I will try at least to
compassionate Thee, * to give Thee thanks, * to
ask of Thee pardon and contrition. * Wherefore, *
with heart and lips I say:

Leader:— *To the Wound of the Left Foot.*

All:—

Ƌoly Wound * of the Left Foot of my Jesus, * I
adore Thee! * I compassionate Thee, * O my
Jesus, * for that most bitter pain which Thou didst
suffer. * I thank Thee for the love * whereby Thou
wast wearied in overtaking me * on the way to ruin, *
and didst bleed amid the thorns and brambles of my
sins. * I offer to the Eternal Father * the pain and
love of Thy most sacred humanity, * in atonement
for my sins, * all of which I detest * with sincere
and bitter contrition.

Leader:— *To the Wound of the Right Foot.*

All:—

Ƌoly Wound * of the Right Foot of my Jesus, * I
adore Thee! * I compassionate Thee, * O my
Jesus, * for that most bitter pain * which Thou
didst suffer. * I thank Thee for the love which pierced
Thee * with such torture and shedding of blood *
in order to punish my wanderings * and the guilty
pleasures I have granted to my passions. * I offer to
the Eternal Father * all the pain and love of Thy
most sacred humanity, * and I pray unto Him for

grace to weep * over my transgressions with burning tears, * and to enable me * to persevere in the
good which I have begun, * without ever swerving
again from my obedience * to the commandments
of my God.

Leader:—To the Wound of the Left Hand.

All:—

Holy Wound * of the Left Hand of my Jesus, * I adore
    Thee! * I compassionate Thee, * O my Jesus,
* for that most bitter pain which Thou didst suffer.
* I thank Thee for having, * in Thy love, * spar-
ed me the scourges and eternal damnation * which
my sins have merited. * I offer to the Eternal Father * the pain and love of Thy most sacred humanity, * and I pray Him to teach me * how to turn
to good account my span of life, * and bring forth in
it worthy fruits of penance, * and so disarm * the
angry justice of my God.

Leader:—To the Wound of the Right Hand.

All:—

Holy Wound * of the Right Hand of my Jesus, *
    I adore Thee! * I compassionate Thee, * O my
Jesus, * for that most bitter pain which Thou didst
suffer. * I thank Thee * for Thy graces lavished on
me with such love, * in spite of all my miserable ob-
stinacy. * I offer to the Eternal Father * all the
pain and love of Thy most sacred humanity, * and
I pray Him * to change my heart and its affections,

* and make me do all my actions * in accordance with the will of God.

Leader:— *To the Wound of the Sacred Side.*

All:—

Holy Wound * in the Side of my Jesus, * I adore Thee! * I compassionate Thee, * O my Jesus, for the cruel insult Thou didst suffer. * I thank Thee, * my Jesus, * for the love which suffered Thy Side and Heart to be pierced, * that the last drops of blood and water might issue forth, * making my redemption to abound. * I offer to the Eternal Father this outrage, * and the love of Thy most sacred humanity, * that my soul * may enter once for all into that most loving Heart, * eager and ready to receive the greatest sinners, * and from it may never more depart. *

——— * ———

Sweet Heart of my Jesus, * grant that I may ever love Thee * more and more.

Leader:— ALL STAND.

PRAYER FOR INCREASE OF DAILY HOLY COMMUNIONS

All:—

O Sweetest Jesus, * Who camest into this world * to give to all the life of Thy grace, * and Who, * to preserve and sustain it, * didst will to be the remedy of our daily infirmities, * and our daily food; * humbly we pray Thee, * by Thy Heart, * all on fire for love of us, * to pour out Thy Holy

Spirit upon all, * so that those who are unhappily in mortal sin * may be converted to Thee, * and recover the life of grace which they have lost; * and those who by Thy gift * still live this divine life, * may every day, * when they are able, * approach devoutly to Thy holy table, * where, * in daily Holy Communion, * receiving every day * the antidote to their daily venial sins, * and nourishing the life of grace in their hearts, * and purifying more and more their souls, * they may come at last * to the enjoyment with Thee of eternal beatitude. * Amen. *

Heart of Jesus. * *burning with love for us,* * *inflame our hearts with love of Thee.*

Leader:— ALL KNEEL.

PRAYER FOR THOSE IN THEIR LAST AGONY

All:—

O Most Merciful Jesus, * Lover of Souls: * I pray Thee, * by the agony of Thy most Sacred Heart, * and by the sorrows of Thy Immaculate Mother, * cleanse in Thy blood * the sinners of the whole world * who are now in their agony * and are to die this day. * Amen. *

Heart of Jesus Agonizing, * *have mercy on the dying.*

Jesus, Mary, Joseph.

Leader:—

PRAYERS FOR THE HOLY FATHER

All:—

O God, * the Shepherd and Ruler of all the faithful, * look down with favor upon Thy servant, * N, * whom Thou hast deigned to appoint * the supreme Pastor of Thy Church; * grant, we beseech Thee, * that both his word and example * may benefit those over whom he has been placed, * so that * together with the flock entrusted to his care * he may attain unto life everlasting, * through Christ our Lord. * Amen. *

Most Sacred Heart of Jesus, * pour in richest fullness * Thy blessings upon Holy Church, * the Pope, and all the clergy; * grant perseverance to the just, * conversion to sinners; * enlighten the unbelievers; * bless our relatives, * friends, * and benefactors; * assist the dying; * deliver the souls in purgatory; * and extend over all hearts * the gentle dominion of Thy love. *

*Lord Jesus, shelter our Holy Father the Pope * under the protection of Thy Sacred Heart. * Be Thou his light, * his strength * and his consolation.*

Leader:—

PRAYER FOR PEACE

All:—

Lord, * make me an instrument of your peace! * Where there is hatred — let me sow love. * Where there is injury — pardon. * Where there is doubt — faith. *

Where there is despair — hope. *
Where there is darkness — light. *
Where there is sadness — joy. *

O Divine Master, * grant that I may not so much seek *
To be consoled — as to console, *
To be understood — as to understand, *
To be loved as to love, * for *
It is in giving — that we receive, *
It is in pardoning — that we are pardoned, *
It is in dying — that we are born to eternal life. *

—— ✠ ——

Saint Francis of Assisi.

B*y the sign of the Holy Cross, * deliver us
from our enemies, * O our God!*

Leader:—

PRAYER FOR MERCY FOR THE HOLY SOULS IN PURGATORY

All:—

Have Mercy, * O gentle Jesus! * on the souls detained in purgatory. * Thou Who for their ransom * didst take upon Thyself our human nature * and suffer the most cruel death, * pity their sighs and the tears shed * when they raise their longing eyes toward Thee; * and by virtue of Thy Passion, * cancel the penalty due to their sins. * May Thy Blood, * O tender Jesus, * Thy Precious Blood, * descend into purgatory * to solace and refresh those who there languish in captivity. * Reach forth Thy hand to them, * and lead them * into the realms of refreshment, * light and peace. * Amen. *

—— ✠ ——

D*ivine Heart of Jesus, * convert sinners, * save the dying, * set free the holy souls in purgatory.*

Leader:—

PRAYER FOR OUR DAILY NEGLECTS

All:—

E*ternal Father, * I offer Thee the Sacred Heart of Jesus, * with all Its love, * suffering and merits: **

All:—

First—To expiate all the sins I have committed this day * and during all my life. *

Leader:— Glory be to the Father, and to the Son, and to the Holy Spirit.

All:— As it was in the beginning, is now, and ever shall be: world without end. Amen.

All:—

Second—To purify the good * I have done badly this day * and during all my life. *

Leader:— Glory be to the Father, and to the Son, and to the Holy Spirit.

All:— As it was in the beginning, is now, and ever shall be: world without end. Amen.

All:—

Third—To supply for the good I ought to have done, * and that I've neglected, * this day and during all my life. *

Leader:— Glory be to the Father, and to the Son, and to the Holy Spirit.

All:— As it was in the beginning, is now, and ever shall be: world without end. Amen.

——— ✠ ———

O *Heart of Love,* * *I put all my trust in Thee,* * *for I fear all things from my own weakness,* * *but I hope for all things from Thy goodness.*

St. Margaret Mary Alacoque

————— ✠ —————

Leader:—

PERIOD OF SILENT ADORATION

"Speak, Lord, for Thy servant heareth."
(1 Kings 3. 10.)

"Lord, what wilt Thou have me do?"
(Acts 9. 6.)

————— ✠ —————

Leader:—

PRAYER FOR FINAL PERSEVERANCE

All:—

O Jesus, * my Savior, * my God, * by Thy Sacred Heart, * by the most pure Heart of the Virgin Mother, * by whatever is pleasing to Thee in heaven and on earth, * I beg and entreat Thee, * grant me holy perseverance, * grant me patience. * Give me grace and courage * that I may efficaciously employ the means which Thou hast given. *

————— ✠ —————

Say three times:—

S *weet Heart of Jesus,* * *be my love,* *

S *weet Heart of Mary,* * *be my salvation.* *

Leader:—

CLOSING PRAYER TO THE BLESSED SACRAMENT

All:—

As this hour of adoration closes, O Jesus, * I renew my faith and trust in Thee. * I am refreshed after these moments with Thee, * and I count myself among a privileged number, * even as Thy disciples were, * who shared Thy actual presence. *

Realizing that my visit to Thee is of little avail * unless I try to live a better life and set a better example, * I am resolved to go forth again to my duties and my concerns * with a renewed spirit of perseverance and good will. * In my daily life I will try to love and serve God well, * and love my neighbor also, * for these two things go together. * I will try to be a true disciple, indeed. * Help me, O Jesus, * in this my resolution. *

Bless me, dear Lord, before I go. * And bless not me alone, O Lord, * but all as well who are here present, * and all who could not come, * especially the sick and the dying. * Bless our homes and all the children there. * Bless all our life and the hour of our death. *

Grant rest to the souls of the faithful departed, * and bring them into the light of Thy divine glory. * So may we who have worshipped Thee * and been blessed by Thee here on earth, * come to behold the radiant glory * of Thy unveiled countenance in heaven for ever and ever. * Amen. *

Say three times:—

Sacred *Heart of Jesus, * Thy Kingdom come!*

Leader:—
FOR THE INTENTIONS OF THE HOLY FATHER TO GAIN THE INDULGENCES OF THE HOLY HOUR

1 Our Father — 1 Hail Mary — 1 Glory be to the Father, etc.

———— ✠ ————

All:—

O *Sacrament most holy, * O Sacrament divine!* * All praise and all thanksgiving * be every moment Thine!*

All:—

In the Name of the Father,✠ and of the Son, and of the Holy Spirit. Amen.

———— ✠ ————

HOLY HOUR INDULGENCES

All those who assist at the Holy Hour of Adoration gain a Plenary Indulgence under the conditions of Sacramental Confession, Eucharistic Communion, and prayers for the intention of the Holy Father.

(Enchiridion of Indulgences, Vatican 1968)

Nihil Obstat–
    John J. Clifford, S. J.
        Censor Liborum

Imprimatur–
    + Samuel A. Stritch,
December 17, 1943   Archbishop of Chicago

Copyright 2001   Soul Assurance Prayer Plan
                  with permission   (TM)
                  CMJ Marian Publishers
                  P.O. Box 661
                  Oak Lawn, IL 60454

Toll Free: 888-636-6799
Office: 708-636-2995
Fax: 708-636-2855
Web Page: www.cmjbooks.com
Email: jwby@aol.com

        ISBN#: 1-891280-39-2